Preschool at Home
Lots of Shapes

Put it all Together

Sue Ozzard

JAPANESE/ENGLISH

Early Childhood Learning Japanese/English Series

mail@early-years.net

copyright© Sue Ozzard & Colin Veryard
All rights reserved.

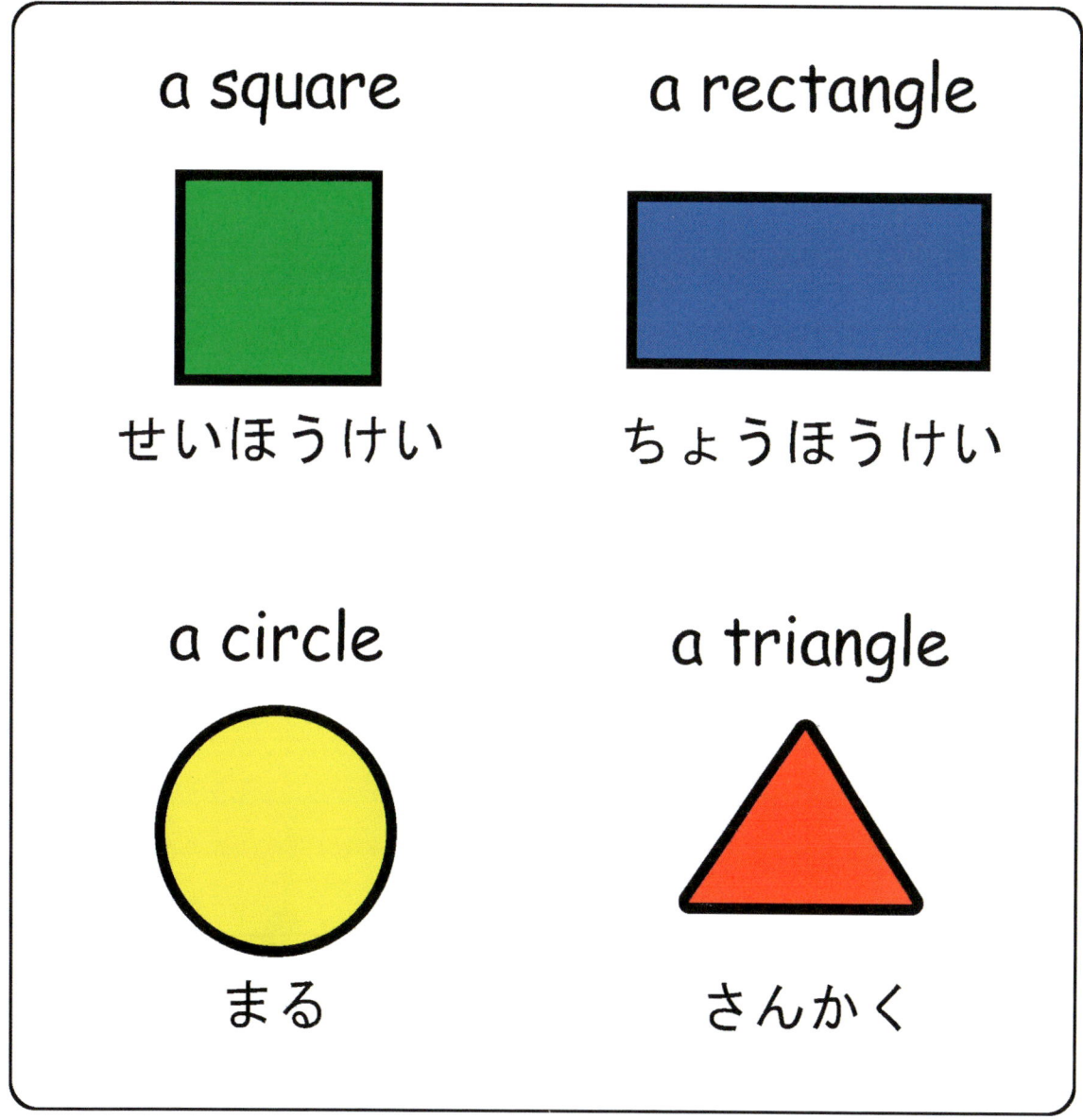

Can you name these shapes?

ここにあるかたちをいってみよう。

2 (two) white ovals

しろのタマゴがたが2つ（ふたつ）

4 (four) brown semi-circles

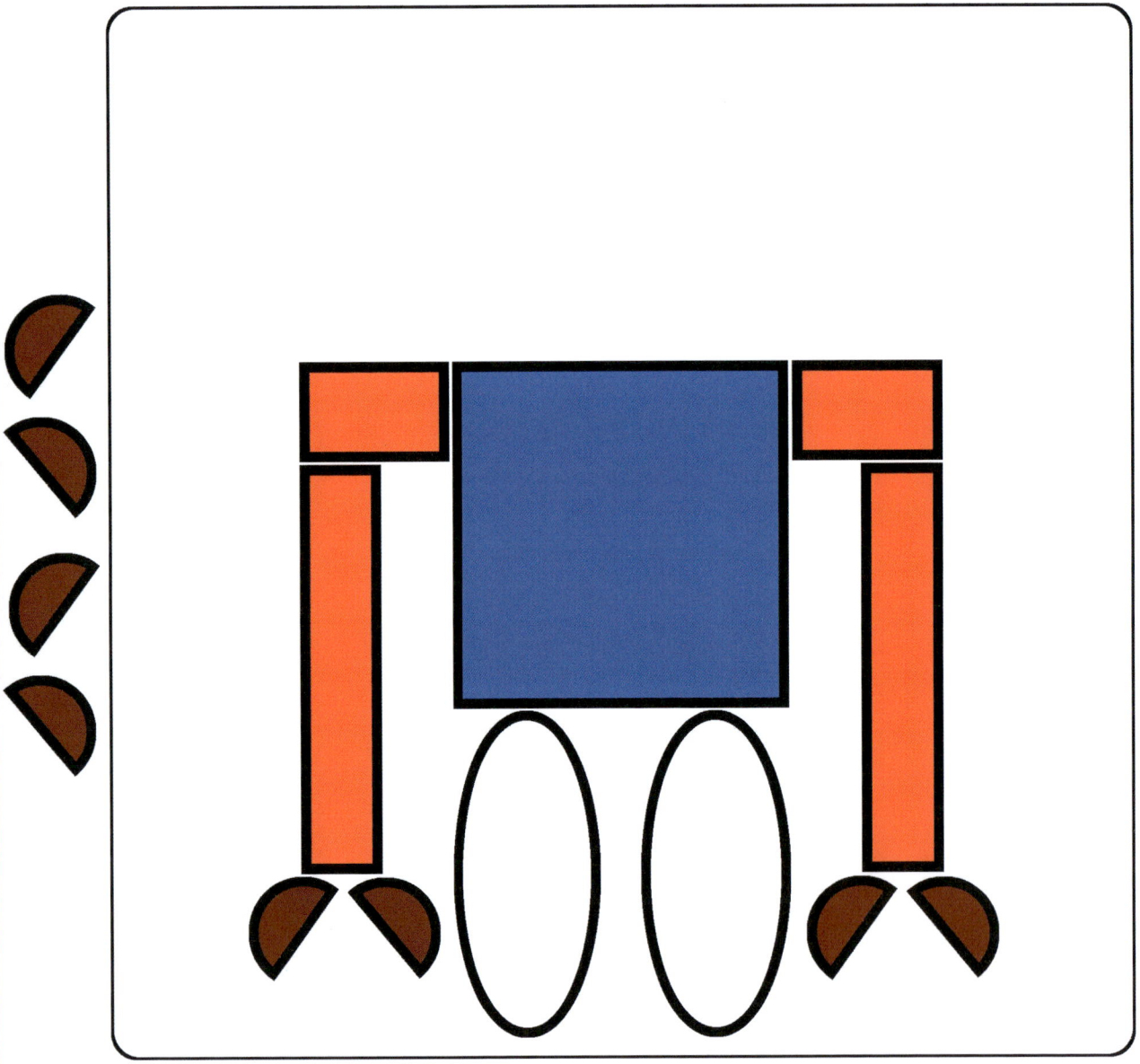

ちゃいろのはんえんが4つ（よっつ）

1 (one) red heart

あかのハートがたが１つ（ひとつ）

1 (one) green diamond

みどりのひしがたが１つ（ひとつ）

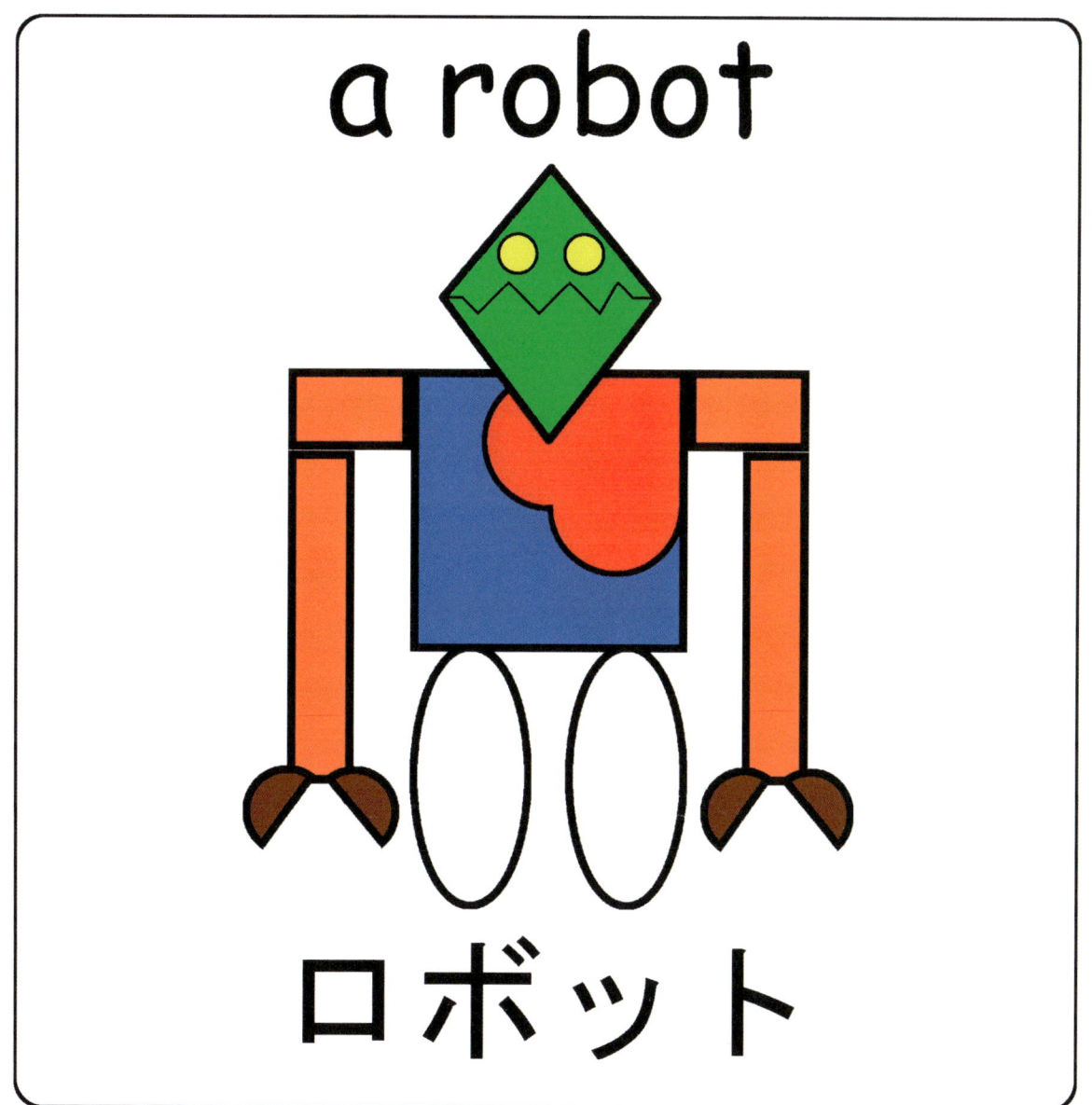

What's happening?

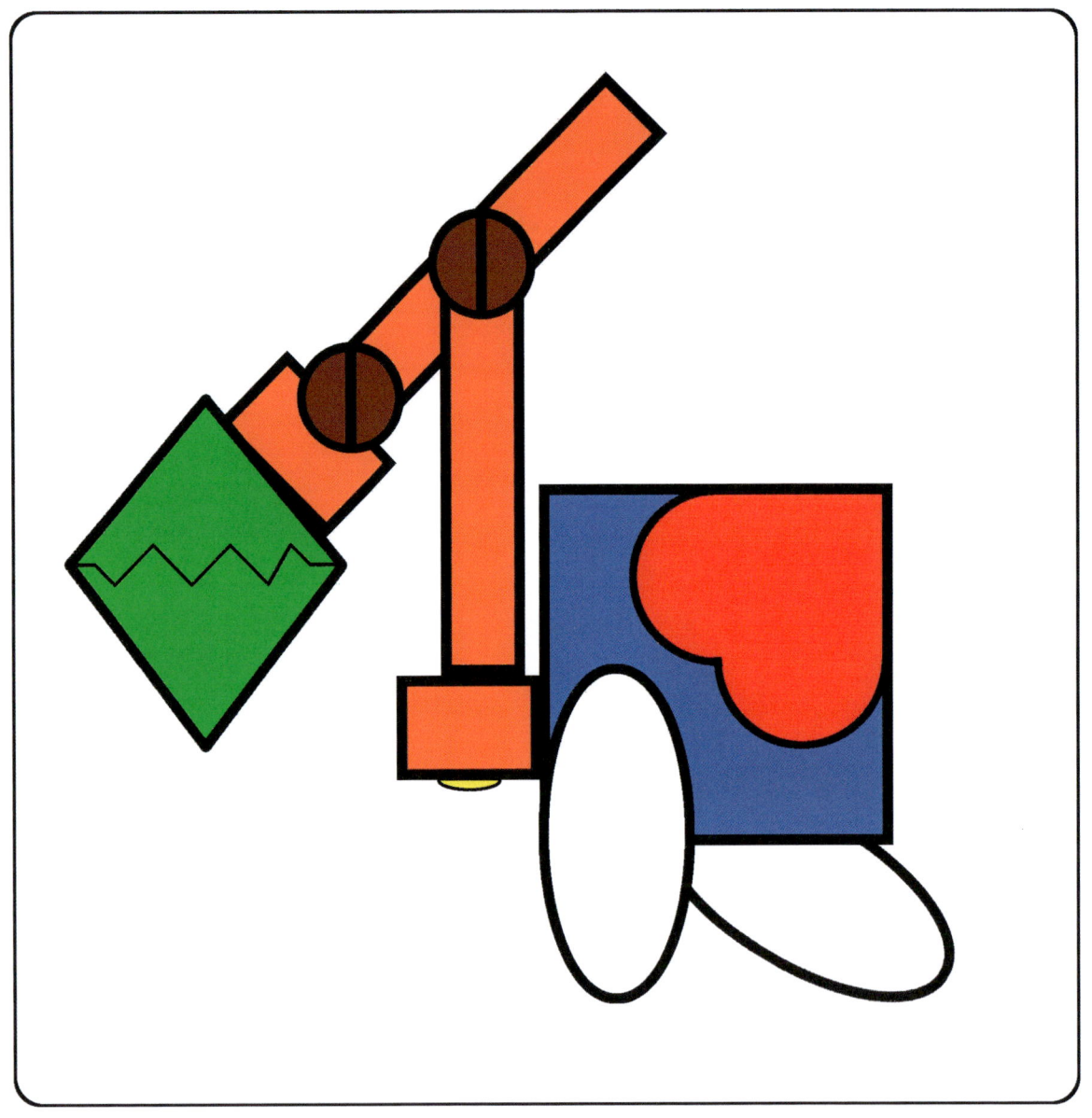

あれ、どうしたのかな?

Are any shapes missing?

たりないかたちはあるかな?

Let's look for some shapes.

もっと、いろんなかたちをみてみよう。

Can you see 4 (four) red hearts?

4つ（よっつ）のあかいハートがたがみえるかな?

Can you see 2 (two) pink semi-circles?

2つ（ふたつ）のピンクのはんえんがみえるかな?

How many oval shapes can you see?

タマゴがたはなんこある?

Can you see 3 (three) green triangles?

3こ（さんこ）のみどりのさんかくがみえるかな?

How many diamond shapes can you find?

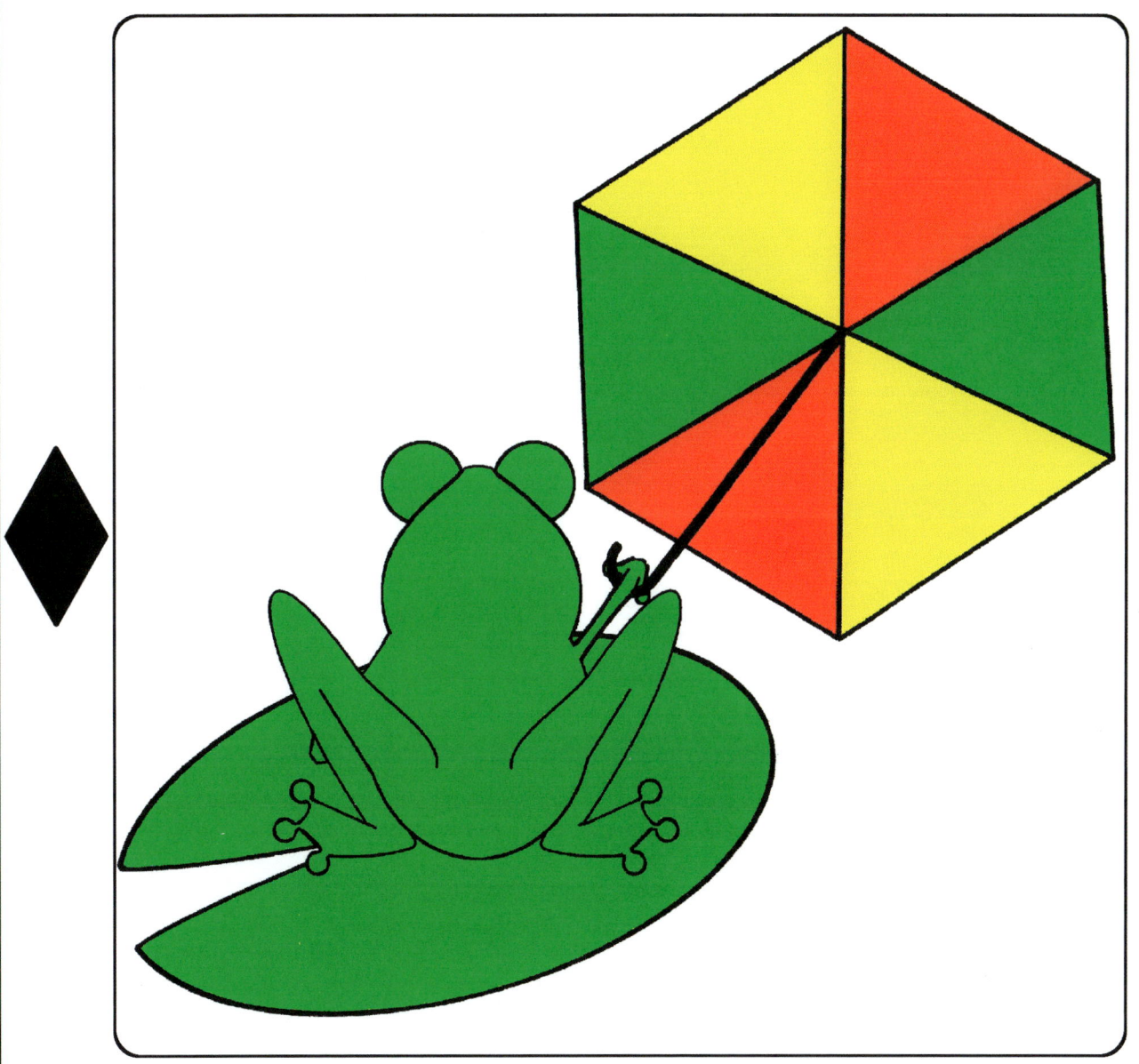

ひしがたはなんこある?

What happened?

あれ、どうしたのかな?

How many semi-circles can you count?

はんえんは なんこあるかな?

Can you see a big circle?

おおきなまるがみえるかな?

How does a pink elephant make oval shapes?

ピンクのゾウさんは、どうやってはんえんをつくったの?

What do you get when an elephant sits on a square?

ゾウさんがしかくにすわると どうなるかな?

What do you get when you cut a circle in half?

まるをはんぶんにしたら なにができる？

What shapes can you see here?

ここには どんなかたちがみえるかな？

What shapes can you see now?

いま どんなかたちがみえるかな?

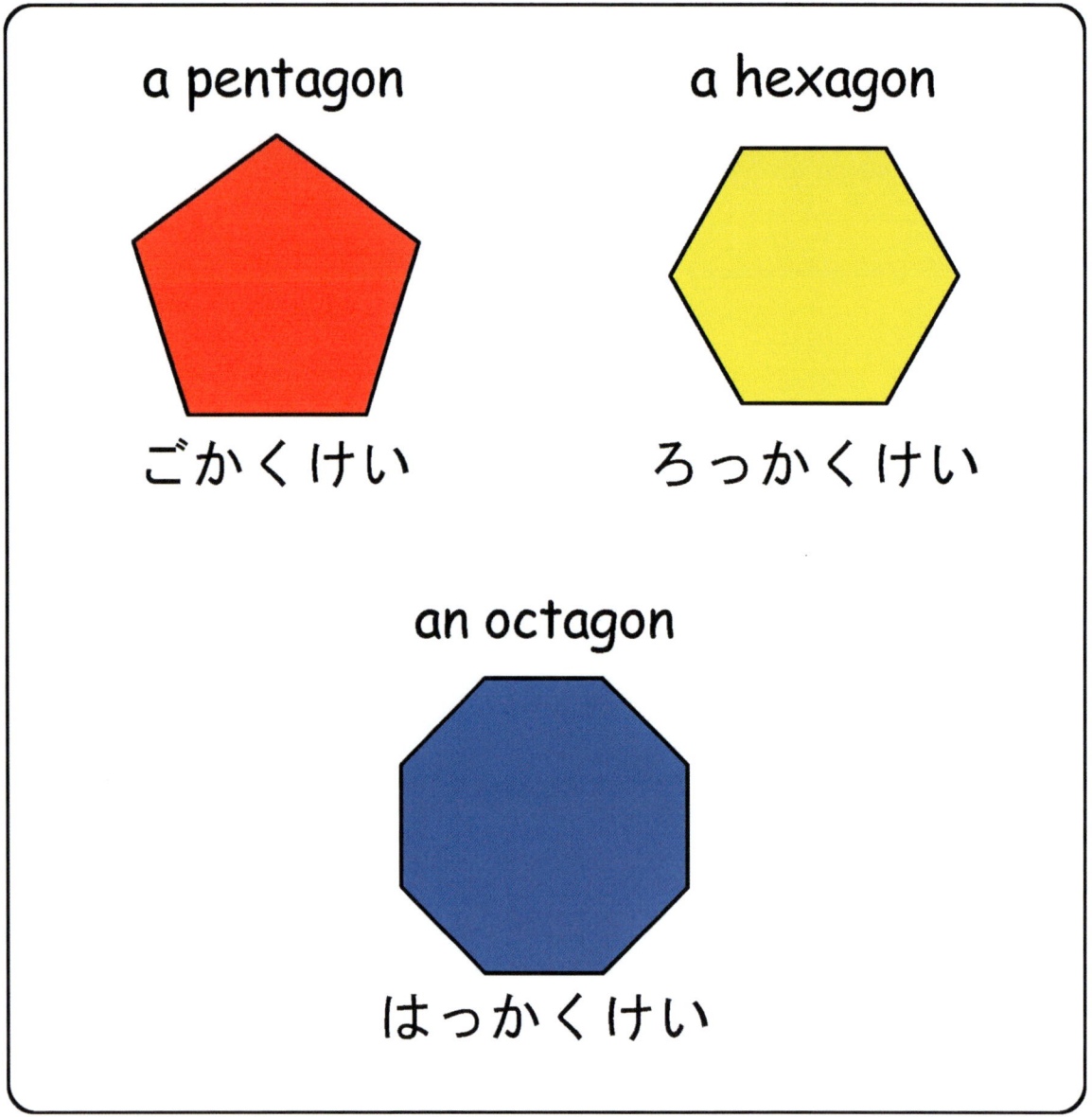

Can you find a hexagon and a pentagon?

ろくかっけいとごかくけいが みえるかな？

What shapes can you see here?

ここには どんなかたちがあるかな?

What shapes can you see now?

いま どんなかたちがみえるかな?

What do you think the numbers mean?

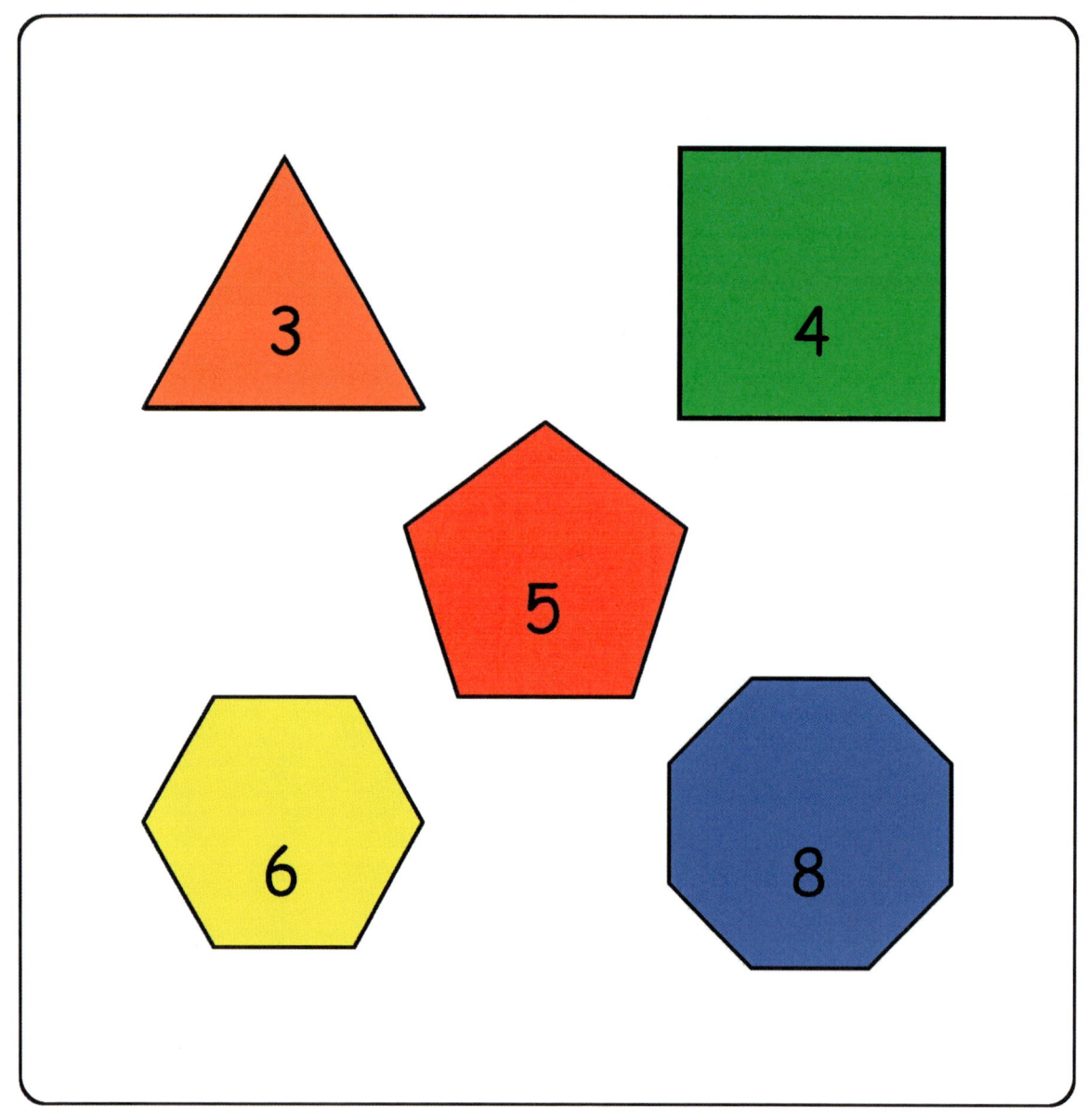

すうじには どんないみがあるのかな?